Faramarz Moazzami

Collected Poems

Thoughts and more

Omslag: Tony Somwang

Culture and Theatre Association "Santra"
Bokpress: BoD - Bok on Demand,
Norderstedt, Germany

ISBN:978-91-89171-10-7

Only you

Naked

Dreams

Thoughts

Light and darkness

In the garden of love

Only you

Poems by

Faramarz Moazzami

Only you

You,

I should love for all my life.

Both when there is sun

and

when there is rain.

Both when there is hot

or

when there is cold.

During

spring and summer,

and

autumn and winter.

You,

I should love for all my life.

Both when I am happy

or

when I am sad.

Both when I am rich

or

when I am poor.

You,

I should love for all my life.

Both when I am awake

or

when I am sleeping.

In reality

or

in my dreams.

You,

I should love for all my life.

Only you

Adore

You,

I should adore.

Like the gods,

who adored Aphrodite.

Before she came to earth,

and became a woman.

You,

I should adore.

Like Adam,

who adored Eve.

Before she left paradise.

You,

I should adore.

Only you

Kiss

I am going to kiss you softly.

As I kiss all the small flowers.

With smell inside my body.

I am going to kiss you softly.

As the tears on the roses.

On your lips and mine.

Soft on soft.

I am going to kiss you softy.

As the sea drops on your body.

Aphrodite song.

I am going to kiss you softly.

Follow

I follow the sun,

as the sun follows me.

I follow the sky,

as the sky follows me.

I follow the earth,

as the earth follows me.

My shadow,

in front and behind me.

Your shadow,

in front and behind me.

I follow my memories,

on the sun,

in the sky

and

on the earth.

Follow

To laugh (1)

I laughed.

She laughed too.

And the children laughed.

The lovers,

hand in hand,

laughed.

The birds sang.

The sun shone.

I looked into her eyes,

they laughed,

and I laughed too.

I looked at her lips,

they laughed,

and I laughed too.

And life laughed with both of us.

Laugh

I,

I,

a wandering soul,

prisoner in my shell.

A shell beyond me.

I,

an unanswered love,

in a galaxy,

which borders on,

infinity and nothing.

I,

a light,

via a glass,

dissolve by sunlight.

I,

a pencil,

which becomes,

smaller and smaller,

with words.

Words,

which turn pale with time.

Time which repeats via glass,

in the galaxy,

out of my shell.

I.

To laugh (2)

In our life,

we laugh at our misery.

While the others,

just cry at it.

It is our way,

to live our life.

To laugh

To cry

I am crying,

because the light day,

became the dark night.

Because,

the red roses faded and withered.

Because,

of a broken heart.

Because,

of the little children,

who became big.

Because of the stars,

which exploded.

Left is my tears,

which are already wiped away.

To cry

Life

Life,

came as the wind,

one day,

and disappeared,

another.

To nothing.

Life,

came as a flame,

one day,

and turned off,

another day.

When it was finished

or

by somebody else.

Somebody

near

or

far away.

Life,

like water in the river,

flowed,

and at the end,

found its way,

to the sand.

Life

Water

We come and go,

like the river.

Sometimes we are calm,

and

sometimes violent.

Like a torrent,

from mountain to valley.

On its way,

it makes and kills the life.

We plant and plunder.

We give and take.

We are a part of nature.

and nature is a part of us.

Water

Particles

Life is composed of,

dark and light particles.

Think,

if you could erase,

the dark particles,

as you wipe,

the words from a blackboard,

from the inside world.

School.

Black particles

I do not exist

I do not exist.

I am only a light.

A reflection.

I am the moon,

on the dark side.

I am the sun,

at the solar eclipse.

I am the star,

under cloud.

I am love,

under hate.

I am an unwritten poem,

and

a song without music.

I,

just do not exist.

If!

If you come,

I am there.

If you do not come,

I am still there.

There is my light.

There is my shadow.

There is my wind.

Everything is there.

As the smell of a flower.

As a picture of the moon,

on sunlight.

And as a memory.

If!

Miss

You are going to miss it.

Again, and again.

The same procedure,

all the time.

Circle,

which becomes smaller and smaller.

The rope,

pulls harder and harder.

Nobody wins.

You lose.

You are on the periphery.

Soon you find yourself in the centre.

Like a point.

Or on the contrary,

you become a line,

on the ground.

Points on the line move.

Overlapping.

They become,

only one point.

Finishing point.

You miss.

To love music

A person who does not love music,

does not love life either.

A person who does not hear,

is deaf or,

has music in her heart.

A person who is away,

hears music with the wind.

Music is a metaphor.

Childrens laughter and sounds are music,

as well as,

the wind singing,

and

the sound of the waves.

The sounds from leaves and birds,

are music,

as well as,

mans praying and complaining.

To love music,

is to love life.

That day

I don't know what your name is.

I don't know what you are doing.

I only see you sometimes.

Your beautiful eyes shine,

it burns and goes deep to my heart.

You don't want to talk with me.

You don't want to know about me.

You are a proud woman,

Like the old Grecian God Aphrodite.

But all Gods come someday to the earth

and

become human being.

I am waiting for that day.

That day will come.

Perhaps!

That day

You are a pretty woman,

and

I am just,

a picture of a man

Naked

Poems by

Faramarz Moazzami

Naked (1)

The clouds flew,

and took your clothes.

The rain dropped on your back.

And the sun shone through the drops on your
nipples.

When you stretched your hand to the water,

removed rainbow through your red cheek,

to the naked blue eyes.

And everything floated in a half green circle.

In our universe is everything naked.

Those who are not naked,

are shadows from the past and the future.

The lies.

Rotating bodies and ponds,

are angels of demons.

Those who are afraid of everything naked in

universe.

Naked truth

The naked truth was you,

as naked as my hands,

stretched to the wind.

The untouchable.

And as naked as the children,

in daddy's embrace.

Heat and coldness,

moved to the heart.

Closely

Naked bodies,

closely together.

Breathing deeply.

Vibration.

Feeling and heat.

Nerves in hands.

Lips and tongue.

And movement towards the universe.

Naked (2)

Naked you went into the water,

before you swam to your destiny.

The light and the dark.

Swane hid your naked body.

And your pains dropped down from your white
skin,

which was black.

Like the fish,

under your feet.

Naked (3)

You were naked,

that day you were born.

Clean as the blood.

You were naked,

that day I touched you.

Clean as the love.

And you will be naked that day you die.

Clean as the soil.

Naked (4)

Naked face.

Lips as free as the red bird.

Kisses sign on your throat.

Shoulder,

like embracing naked pitchers.

Breasts,

like mountains at sunset.

Belly,

like the earth under devil's look.

Legs,

like palm threes.

And footprints on the sand,

waiting for your naked body.

Every drop of body,

was a light sign.

And the eyes,

were stars in the enormous universe.

With the white bird's sound vibration,

at the vacuum.

Naked (5)

You were naked with clothes on.

Your eyes gave the sign.

And your hands which moved into the air,

showed things which don't exist.

Naked (6)

Naked were the body and the light.

Naked were the white,

the yellow, the red and the black.

Naked were the words,

which burned the brain and changed it to the
body.

And naked was the soul.

Unsealed.

I am the queen of the light,

and

the king of the darkness.

I am the sun and the moon,

in the same body and soul.

Naked thoughts

Nobody could read my naked thoughts.

Though,

they were as naked as Aphrodite,

in the Greek sea.

With water drops on her body.

Drops that flew down.

And thoughts that disappeared.

She was God.

And the thoughts are always divinely,

how devilish they are.

Naked thoughts

When the darkness falls,

becomes everything naked.

Bodies,

thoughts,

and the light,

In the darkness.

Dreams

Poems of

Faramarz Moazzami

Dreams (1)

Pretty woman,

who only dreams.

And we men,

stand besides,

knowing nothing about her dreams.

We want to be in her dreams.

At least in a part of them.

But we can`t.

We are gone.

Away with our own.

Two dreams which should parry.

Tangents in life.

But it doesn't.

Because they are just dreams.

Like an echo of sound.

Far away from reality.

Only waves.

Rings on water,

and then still.

Still nights.

Furious nights.

The nights the shadows,

the lights, move.

We became shadows in the periphery,

there happens nothing.

Just nothing.

Far away is life.

Only one time only.

Dreams

Spring (1)

Soon is spring here,

with your heat.

And I,

as cold as the winter wind,

and

ice.

Waiting for heat,

and you.

Spring

What am I doing here?

What am I doing here?

A question.

Again, and again.

Where is here?

My home?

My country?

The earth?

The universe?

Everything diffuses in human being life.

Boring time gives thoughts about life.

We live,

and we think.

Or

we think,

because we live.

Philosophy,

and its boring phraseology.

Up too simple and difficult.

To hit us with a weep.

An invisible weep.

Truth!

What is truth?

What am I doing here?

Noora

She was Noor,

light.

Beautiful and virgin.

The light broke my heart.

Thawed the ice.

And I was there,

warm as a fool.

Who could not do anything.

The kisses and caresses were thousands.

And the life flew,

as quick as a bird.

That I couldn't notice things that exist,

and don't exist.

And I was there,

there I was before,

at periphery.

But now near the centre.

Noora

I saw

I saw her.

She walked on the street,

and

in my dreams.

She saw me too.

But she did not.

Did she or not?

In my dream,

I saw her.

You

You went,

and I was there.

Lonely in crowd.

With my heart,

with the pounding.

Waiting.

My hands stretched,

seeking the sun.

The untouchable.

And love like a story,

told thousands of times,

of Scheherazade.

Waiting.

Love like a poem,

written on clouds,

and gone with winds,

and you.

Way

I saw in her eyes her desperation,

because of me.

I became an evil one.

In a sequence of pride,

I forget who I was.

Power,

as a pyramid of glass.

As fragile as small veins,

around the heart.

And the cells in my brain.

The time of self-analysis.

Sad, I backed,

from the way that was my way but still no way.

The life was her way.

And there I stood.

Way

Waiting

Waiting in bus station.

Waiting outside the cinema.

Waiting for spring.

Waiting for love.

Waiting to see the sea.

Waiting to see Spain.

Waiting,

longing to feel something else.

Waiting,

yearning to feel something else.

The continuous longing.

The time passed.

And the end.

Waiting

Lonely

I am lonely,

with my mind

and

my feeling.

With my soul

and

my heart.

I hear my heart.

I hear the clock.

I am lonely,

I hear the wind.

I hear the song of the bird.

I hear dancing leaves.

I am lonely,

with my mind.

With my feeling.

With my heart

and

With my soul.

Lonely

She

Who was she?

Body

or

soul?

Her way to go,

But was she reality,

or

fantasy?

Was she autumn,

or

winter?

None of them.

She was spring.

She was smelled of spring flowers.

She was summer.

She was summer heat.

She was both body and soul.

She was both thinking and fantasy.

She was love.

Oh darling

Oh darling

You are in the blue room,

there heavens gates are open,

and the sea is naked.

Oh darling

You are in the green room,

there the birds are on the trees,

and the nightingale is singing.

Oh darling

You are in the red room,

there the blood incites you,

and the red apple,

is on your chin and your lips.

Oh darling

You are in the white room,

there the reality and fantasy are mixed.

And I am in the dark room,

there the light is off.

Waiting for the gates of four heaven ascensions
to open.

Oh darling

Children

Children laughed,

I laughed too.

They were angels,

with wings.

But my wings were broken.

They were children.

They were free,

but I was a slave.

I was a prisoner.

They run,

but my foots were bound.

They played hide and seek,

but I was afraid of the darkness.

Children laughed,

I laughed too,

and life laughed at me.

Human being

I am a human being.

What am I?

Who am I?

What am I doing?

Am I living?

or

I am dead.

Questions are many,

answers are few.

I laugh.

I am a human being,

but am I plant,

or

soil?

What am I?

Who am I?

What am I doing?

I am a human being.

Traveller

I am always a traveller.

I pass countries and cities.

I am a traveller.

I pass mountains,

seas and deserts.

I am a traveller.

Sometimes I stay.

Sometimes I make love.

I am a traveller.

Sometimes I want to comeback.

Sometimes I want to forget.

I am a traveller.

A traveller of life.

Short and long journeys.

Beginning and ending.

Beginning,

Life.

Ending,

Death.

I am a traveller.

A traveller of life.

Traveller

Soon

Soon is man dead.

Dead, dead as long time ago.

Soon is man away,

away in eternity,

at the side of universe.

Soon is man sand,

sand around Jupiter,

beside the mountain.

Soon, soon,

and then there is nothing more.

Only nothing.

Soon

I am crazy

I am crazy.

Crazy in life.

Crazy in existence.

It is coming one day,

that I am not exist anymore.

There is no life.

There is no existence and no craziness.

And not me either.

I am crazy.

Spring (2)

It was spring.

There were flowers.

There was rain.

There were birds.

It was love.

But I was lonely.

Why?

I don`t know.

It was spring.

There were nightingales.

It was song.

It was a love song.

But I was not in love.

Why?

I don`t know.

Spring

Dreams (2)

I am dreaming.

In the world of dreams,

I see the sea.

I see the mountains.

I am in the clouds.

I fly.

In the world of dreams,

I am a ship,

on the oceans.

In the world of dreams,

I am in love.

I make love.

I come back from my dreams.

Do I live?

Am I in the world of dreams?

Show me

Show me the world,

then I shall show you the star.

Show me the trees,

then I shall show you the sun.

Show me the birds,

then I shall show you the sea.

Show me your dreams,

then I shall show you the moon.

Show me love,

then I shall show you the universe.

Show me.

Every day

Every day is a beginning and an end.

Every day is a new poem,

an unwritten one.

The light orange of sunrise,

and

the dark orange of sunset.

Love and friendship.

Every day

Thoughts

Poems by

Faramarz Moazzami

I don´t know if I live right or wrong.

I don´t know if I do right or wrong.

Everything is confused.

Everything is absurd.

And

what about the consequence?

Just a light.

Just a song.

Just a heat.

And the heart,

as soft as before

and

as hard as before.

I change nothing.

I do nothing.

And the heart...

Admire the beautiful hair of women.

Red colour,

as the rose.

Black colour,

as the night.

And the blond colour,

as the day,

the sun.

Long hair,

to take me up to your heart.

The sun

He cried and cried.

Where is my flower?

Where is my flower?

He went around and looked after it.

You can buy a new one.

The shop is not open right now,

perhaps tomorrow.

But he continued to search.

After a while,

he sat and spoke.

My flower,

my woman is away.

I went to the end.

There was nothing more and nothing less.

Tell me who I am?

I do always my best,

still, I didn´t succeed.

Where are you?

Where are you?

Just an echo.

Sometimes I went over the border.

Infinity

In my best dream,

I was a dream.

And,

in my worst dream,

I was still a dream.

Time is my enemy,

and

you are my friend.

You were the best part of my life,

the light one.

What did I say to you?

You said nothing!

You just talked.

She said:

You like your money more than me.

Perhaps!

Perhaps not!

I want you for whole night.

She said:

What you need is a wife.

I said:

I had already one.

101

She wanted to be lonely.

The other one,

wanted to go with her.

And the other one,

I don´t know anything about her.

In the beginning,

was everything new,

and everything old.

In the beginning,

was everything new and still old.

Talk with me,

when you know something about yourself.

You know more about me,

than I know about myself.

She is complicated.

But complicated is blocked.

Like the ice.

I want to tell you about me.

No, I don´t want.

I am an animal,

and you are too.

But you think that you are something else.

And else is nothing.

Just a belief.

The beginning was the end.

And the end,

was beginning.

____

You miss me.

And I miss you.

Just a stupid play.

Who need you?

Nobody.

Just a bluff.

In the process of knowing,

you know nothing.

In the process of learning,

you learn nothing.

It is pity,

if you cry more for money,

because I have not any.

My last day was the first,

and

your first day was the last.

My last day was the first,

and

your last day was the last.

I am more interested about myself than you.

Pity.

You want to spend more time with me.

But I am tired of you and of me.

To win and to lose is a bad play.

I want to tell you something about nothing.

I suddenly remarked,

that I never looked at the other side.

It was just a river.

A stationary one.

Poetry is just a dream,

a dream about the truth.

And who interested in dreams?

The nice girls,

like the nice things.

And nothing.

She kissed me on my lips,

and showed the way.

But the way was no way,

just a trouble,

beside the other troubles.

And the way to nothing.

Someone or something was wrong in your life.

And you believed in it.

- - - -

The way we are thinking,

is the way we are living.

We walked together.

But she walked for herself,

and I for myself.

You were my life,

and the life was dead.

You were my destiny,

and destiny was a joke.

You are colder than the cold.

You are interested in me,

but I am not interested in you.

It is always the same,

wherever you go.

You are always the same,

wherever you are.

I made it!

I made it!

But you made nothing.

The visible world was the world,

and the rest was a question.

Everything is part of me,

and nothing is part of you.

I found you on the moon.

You found me on the sun.

You burned,

and

I froze.

The first time I was here,

was the last time.

And the last time I was here,

was the first time.

And the time was relative,

except the first

and

the last one.

I gave you everything.

And what did you give me?

Only disappointment.

135

It is not important what you are,

it is important what you say.

It is not important what you say,

it is important what you are.

Tell me the truth,

then I tell you who you are.

Tell me who you are,

then I tell you the truth.

The way was long,

and you were far away.

Don´t sit on steps,

it is cold.

Sit om my knees.

139

Don´t tell me what you are,

tell me what you have.

Don´t tell me what you have,

tell me what you are.

140

I don´t know,

perhaps I am so intensive,

or on the contrary,

so cold.

Two opposite side of the same world.

My nature.

When the wind is blowing,

in the hot summer,

or

in the cold winter.

You don´t know who I am,

and you never come to know.

Nothing more to do.

Nothing new to say.

Everything is done,

and

everything is said.

I don´t want to hurt you,

I just love you.

And I don´t want that you hurt me,

if you love me.

I am outside,

and you are inside.

And you are outside,

and I am inside.

And we are everywhere and nowhere.

You should not misunderstand me,

I like you so much.

When I ask you something,

I just want to know.

There is no statement.

No judgement.

I don´t mean something special.

I accept you as you are,

and you should accept me as I am.

Remember me as a flower,

faded.

Remember me as a star,

exploded.

And remember me as a sun,

an extinct one

I thought,

I can make a woman of you.

But you were already one.

A special one.

I thought,

I can travel with you.

But you were already gone with yourself.

I thought that I can live with you.

But you had already a life.

A life without anybody.

Nothing I can do,

and everything I do become wrong.

But think if the right is wrong and if the wrong is
right.

And everything is confused.

As the right and the wrong

And how could you totally discard me,

when I totally account on you.

As in a balance.

Balance of the life.

In our nature of the life,

nothing is impossible.

Even dreams.

151

And the sun

is always the sun,

despite the clouds.

But the moon,

is never the moon,

despite the sun.

You were already the second,

when the first was gone.

And when you become the first,

there will be not second.

The kind of love you gave me,

was as narrow as the heart.

And I am going to give you,

nothing more than my heart.

And now,

when everything is finished,

the cold wind is blowing.

And the red sun is shining.

There is two ways to live,

The first is to live,

the second is to die.

There is no more time.

And all the time is other time.

Out of the time.

I want to make you happy,

but I can´t.

I want to satisfy you,

but I can´t.

I want to do everything,

but I can´t.

I can make you naked,

before my eyes.

I can paint on you,

before my eyes.

I can make love with you,

before my eyes.

I can.

You are my dream.

And dream is you.

And everything else is dreams,

except you,

that is my dream.

The life was short,

and still long.

I noticed it when I talked with you.

And when I had my hand in yours.

Heart.

Under the dropping rain.

In the late autumn and early spring.

A witness.

Sometimes I must go outside my dreams.

Inside eternity.

You are always the same,

whatever you are.

Poetry is just a dream.

A dream about the truth.

And who is interested of the dream?

Nothing more to do.

Nothing new to say.

Everything is done,

and

everything is said.

There is always somebody else.

A richer one.

There is always somebody else.

A stranger one.

There is always somebody else.

More beautiful one.

But the sky is sky.

The sea is the sea.

And the earth is the earth.

And you are still living.

The light and darkness

Poems by

Faramarz Moazzami

When the light disappeared,

we were only a repetition of the past.

When the song was finished,

you were a cry.

A question of the particles.

Untouchable.

And the cry was a song for the deaf.

When the light disappeared,

I cried:

Switch on, switch on!

But you slept in the dark.

You were the universe,

but still empty.

Carbohydrate.

Only energy.

Universe is where the love is.

The rest is just an illusion of nothing.

When I moved the cells in my brain one round,

the light came.

But the song disappeared.

You were gone,

with your tail.

The light one.

Which became dark,

as my eyes.

When I disappeared in the deep,

you came to the surface.

You called me.

The birds heard you,

but not me.

You hid yourself,

at the back of the darkness.

And I,

at the back of you.

When all the wise people discussed the questions,

cried the fool,

and it became the silence.

How, how, how?

The sound was inside the tunnel.

As a laser ray.

Where, where, where?

The sound came out from the tunnel,

and burned the greens.

When, when, when?

The sound disappeared to nothing,

through the darkness.

You are just a note,

a short one,

on the light.

In the light and darkness,

was the size,

a sight mistakes.

In the dark days,

I saw the light,

spread in time,

which didn´t exist.

Blind because of the sun.

The biggest of biggest,

was the smallest.

The limit had disappeared long time ago.

In the extreme security,

I was doubtful,

about things that exist.

And in the extreme doubt,

I was sure,

about things that don't exist.

The last song,

was my song,

but still it was,

a beginning to the song.

In my craziest dream,

I was a dream.

In our maximum attempt to get happiness,

we came to the maximum level of unhappiness.

When everything was answered,

somebody asked a question.

The darkness fell.

I analysed everything.

At the end I noticed,

that analyse was wrong.

Everything was as clear as love.

The worst is not things that happen sometimes,

in the darkness.

The worst is the things that happen all the times,

in the light.

She said:

Look at me,

look at me.

I looked at her,

but I saw nothing.

Only a picture,

of something which doesn't exist.

The summation resulted in a minus,

of the meaningless of life.

When the balance was rubbed,

I came in balance,

on a fragile support.

When the wind was blowing at me,

I felt the particles from the past.

And when the wind was blowing at her,

I saw the photons of forgetfulness.

In the headline world,

there was no place for me.

I was forced to change to the next.

I took myself away,

from every corner.

The picture crashed,

at the same moment that eyes closed.

And the rest was found everywhere.

In the eyes of the world,

you are a smell.

Perhaps a light or a song.

But still a question.

When the worst was over,

nothing existed.

Only a melody of desperation.

And when I saw the sun,

I forgot you.

The light was light,

and you were the light.

And I was blind.

When darkness fell,

you were a star.

A light ray.

Out of meaningless,

born the light.

the sky,

the sea,

and

you.

In the love garden

Poems by

Faramarz Moazzami

I was everywhere and nowhere.

I saw you,

in the light of the moon.

The eyes.

Everything diffuses.

And when the night was over,

we were just in the beginning.

Beginning of beginning

and

nothing.

And your eyes were mine,

and my eyes was yours,

and nothing more.

And when the song was finished,

your hands were outstretched,

and wanted to show something.

Something that nobody saw.

Only movement,

and the eyes,

which saw nothing.

Suffer was the word.

The dance began again,

and the movements.

Everybody saw,

and

still nobody.

And you danced so beautiful.

Your hands were still outstretched,

and you prayed.

I saw your beautiful belly,

and your black eyes,

which hide life mysteries.

Cruelty.

We were animals,

and still human being.

When you were in my embrace,

I was in you,

and you were in me.

And when I kissed your necks,

you bit me on my ears.

And I dreamed nothing,

dream was you.

And what did you dream?

Perhaps on me,

Perhaps not!

And when it was over,

you didn´t want to look at my eyes.

I could not see if you were happy or not.

Perhaps it was just lust.

And the lust is the gate to paradise.

The love paradise.

It was pity that there were no birds,

and not either song.

It only blowing.

And you had cold feet and froze.

I should kiss your legs.

and made them warm,

but I didn´t.

We think a lot after,

when everything is over,

in belief that we could do better.

But second are second,

and the taste of kisses is just a memory.

I wanted to forget.

And I do it now.

You came back,

as beautiful as before,

or even more.

I became so happy.

There was a star, the heaviest in my heart.

The dead song.

And it is sad to look at love through sex.

And you could look at my eyes,

through the black hole,

without blunder.

You were strong.

In our dreams,

we saw the end of the world,

nothing, through the eyes,

yours and mine.

You had a whistle,

a special one.

Every time we had nothing to do,

we blow in it.

We created sound of chaos,

the sound of the life.

And you painted for me,

for that bloody stupid,

which was still kind enough to understand.

You were naked and looked at me.

Somebody was afraid.

It was you or me?

The music was on, and it was high.

I doubted,

or perhaps you did?

The next seconds you rushed to me and took me.

We were in heaven.

You were there on the bed,

like the queen of Saba and cried.

If it was because of music,

or it was something else,

it was difficult for me to know.

I was stupid as usual and didn´t understand.

No, I understood,

but I played I didn´t.

Deep feelings are nothing for me.

It is like to sink in an abyss,

heaven.

I want to have control on my feelings,

and I want to cry lonely,

on my dreams.

Perhaps you wanted that I kiss you but I didn´t.

You lied there a little time with close eyes.

You perhaps pretend that you slept.

After a while you went up and went home.

And I was tired.

I wanted to forget everything.

Only to sleep was my song.

I was there and saw you.

I kissed your cheek.

You remember me from the heat of the kiss.

And I still feel the taste of the kiss.

It was just a second.

I still wanted to come to you,

but I didn´t.

I only looked at you and moved away.

Out of the sight,

and trough the time.

And you were happy and I too.

Until I became sad,

as a drop of rain in the autumn darkness,

before it touches the sea,

you.

Through the winds,

and the dreams.

When the music was off,

you imitated me.

My hands were yours.

And when the music was on,

you sat sad,

in your dreams

I wanted to kiss you,

and I did.

You said nothing and showed nothing.

Sometimes you laughed,

and again, you were in your dreams.

I tried to catch them,

but unsuccessful.

It was as impossible as to imitate my hands.

And you went away without to say a word.

Not either to say goodbye.

In your wordless world, quiet with music on.

The birds sung,

and you my darling was gone.

I was tired of you,

and you were tired of me.

I saw the light,

and you saw darkness.

The birds lived and we saw nothing.

Vi repeated the non-repeatable.

The red flowers became evident in the green
field.

And the clouds flied,

parallel with all not visible.

Your lips which was so soft and so beautiful,
was not there.

And your tongue which burned my heart, too.

It was not love,

but still it was.

And all songs remained there,

in the flowers smell,

and in the birds singing.

Those who live.

It took long time before I saw you.

And when I saw you, it was late,

though it was early.

You laughed and you wanted.

But I was ashamed.

The red colour of the life.

I touched your hair,

and looked at your lips,

and thought about the next time we shall meet.

If we do?

We played and laughed.

We were boxing in the elevator,

and embracing from time to time.

The life was a game for some minutes.

When I touched your breast,

which was as hard as pomegranate,

I had the world in my hand.

And when I sucked it,

I got all worlds blood in me.

And when everything was over,

we were two statues of meat and blood,

waiting för reconciliation.

The sun skinned,

and you slept and slept.

I became more and more worried.

I dreamed bad dreams.

The birds flied high up on the trees.

You slept.

I heard your breathing.

Slowly and slowly.

It made me calm and worried.

I kissed your cheek,

and asked why?

I get no answer.

You breathed more and more deeply,

and slept.

When the heaven was dark

and the wind was cold,

you shined and all became different.

You saw everything,

and I nothing.

And the sun was a fairy,

for those people which could understand and see.

And I,

who wished to make love one more time,

violent and passionate,

before I travel away.

The long journey.

It was you with close eyes.

The tops of fingers,

nails.

And all the kisses.

The air which vibrated as never before.

Before our noses and our ears.

Body to body

and

soul to soul.

And shout to the heaven.

The unbelievable.

A finished song,

which still was unfinished.

And praying to the next sunshine and sunset.

And you gave me creps,

one after one.

And put them in my mouth.

I felt your fingers on my lips.

They were as sweet as the taste of the creps.

And your shining eyes,

as the creps in the sunshine.

We were lying on the sand,

on the beach,

in the early spring,

when the sea was quiet.

The sun shined on my black back,

and

your white breast.

You took away the sands from my back.

Oh.... your hand.

You gave me the rest of creps,

and I kissed you,

and touched your soft lips.

We looked for a while to heaven and the birds,

and all the lovers who passed by,

and kissed each other's.

When I looked at the sea,

you asked me,

" What are you thinking"?

I thought nothing.

It existed only the time being,

and the heaven and the sea,

and you.

After a while,

the shadows took the sun.

And the waves raised.

You froze,

and I.

We went home hand in hand.

When I wanted to make love you didn´t,

and when you want to make love,

I couldn´t

But it came a time,

when the stars shined,

and both of us came to the same course,

in the same galaxy.

There it was everything and nothing.

This time I made your feet warm.

I did it despite that I was tired.

You didn´t notice,

or you pretend.

Perhaps you slept.

When you were warm,

I became warm too,

in my heart.

And I was afraid as usual,

in the time of desperation and misunderstanding.

And when you were with me,

you painted something to me,

and to yourself,

so slowly, so slowly.

I kissed you sometimes.

But you don´t want to become disturb.

You listen to your music.

Somebody made shower,

and somebody else shaved himself.

And all the sounds disappeared in silence.

And I wrote.

We were again on the beach.

The crane played and the sun shined,

on the concrete and on us.

The last heat.

We embraced and kissed each other.

You went proud as a Greece god,

before you disappeared,

somewhere after the way, in the garden of love.

You looked at me and gave me a sign,

when the Greece singer sang.

And you made me lucky.

And the happiness was just a second,

that disappeared with you,

in love garden

The Author

Faramarz Moazzami was born in Iran but is
living in Sweden since 1970.

He was working as an engineer, economist and
teacher.

He has written several books both in Persian and
in Swedish, published in Iran and in Sweden. He
wrote several collections of poems; theatre plays
and novels.

His first poems published in Lyrikvännen in year
2000 and he participated at several poetical
festivals in Stockholm, last time at Poesimässa
(Poesifestival) year 2023.

Collected poems, Thoughts and more are some
examples of his English poems.